ANOTHER MOTHER DOES NOT COME WHEN YOURS DIES

Another Mother Does Not Come When Yours Dies

MUBANGA KALIMAMUKWENTO

WAYFARER BOOKS

ABIQUIÚ, NEW MEXICO

WAYFARER BOOKS

WWW.WAYFARERBOOKS.ORG

All Rights Reserved
Published in 2025 by Wayfarer Books
Cover Design and Interior Design by Connor Wolfe
Cover Image © Annie Spratt
TRADE PAPERBACK 9781965320310

10 9 8 7 6 5 4 3 2 1

Look for our titles in paperback, ebook, and audiobook wherever books are sold.
Wholesale offerings for retailers available through Ingram.

Wayfarer Books is committed to ecological stewardship.
We greatly value the natural environment and invest in conservation.

PO Box 1109, Abiquiú New Mexico

413.441.7003 | orders@homeboundpublications.com

WAYFARERBOOKS.ORG

DEDICATION

For my sister, Nchimunya Anna Kalimamukwento

CONTENTS

Part III

Part IV

Part V

tapafwa noko, apesa umbi
another mother does not come when yours dies

−BEMBA PROVERB

PART I

ANOTHER MOTHER DOES NOT COME WHEN YOURS DIES I

I learn how to pray on my mother's lap. We are at Bible study, as we are every Friday evening in the pastor's house, surrounded by people I see on Fridays and then again on Sundays during the main service. My mother always starts these evenings quiet, only *Shani*-ing and *Bwino, shani*-ing between handshakes with the other adults in a whisper. Then she pulls her concentration face–lips pursed–and nods at everything the pastor says even though he tells zigzagging stories about lips-shut lions, talking shrubs, and direct conversations with God.

The smell of *Eat-Sum-Mor* biscuits and milked tea wafts up from the glass coffee table in the middle of the sitting room. I'm sure everyone's stomach is grumbling, not just mine. But the routine is, no one moves to pick either biscuit or teacup until Amai Busa, the pastor's wife, offers the tray just before we leave when the tea is too cold and the biscuits have hardened around the edges.

The first time we came here, I raised my hand to ask a question. My mother chuckled, pulling it down, telling me afterwards *That's not how things are done*, even though I'd heard her tell the pupils she tutored that, questions were how we learnt.

I want to ask if the lion's mouth was shut with a zipper or a lock, why no one thought to pour water on that poor shrub, and what number is God's because I like memorizing phone numbers. But I remain quiet, remembering how my mother says, *Once is for the instruction, the second will be a slap*, and rub my cheek as if it is already stinging.

My mother has no questions and only breaks her reverie by mouthing her *Amen*. The pastor is talking about a marriage between repentance and forgiveness at this point, explaining that the children of that marriage are blessings like he and his wife enjoy now. He points to the chandelier with its knife-sharp prisms, at their daughter, Hosanna, who is reading a children's Bible next to her mother, and then at his car keys laid next to the biscuits and cooling tea. I watch his fat pointer finger float from blessing to blessing and conjure this God as a fairy, blessing and blessing and blessing.

Amen, goes my mother's mouth. Her breath, still pepperminty because she insists on us brushing our teeth before we leave the house, kisses me lightly on my head.

This sermon—like the ones before—ends with the same series of promises of restoration, that God will rebuild whatever area of our lives had been eaten by termites, the way he did for Joseph and for Hannah and for Jacob and Sarah.

Hallelujah! Preach it! Glory! and *Amen!* jump out from the adults' mouths like fireflies. This is where my mother's voice steps in, warm as freshly fried vitumbuwa, round as the hug she has me enveloped in. She joins in the incantations, the first of the adults to flee English and dip into a language of her own fabrication, but no one minds. They start down parallel paths of gibberish, which my mother told me is called speaking in tongues. I shut my eyes. The way their tongues crash into each other reminds me too much of the rainy season's first thunder, how, even though November petrichor warns of its coming, my heart never fails to jolt at the sound. I always run to hide under the blankets as if they can shield me from the rapid, incessant booming.

The vibrations of my mother's voice through her chest drum against my ears, climbing louder and louder until, just when I think whatever holds sounds in it will split at the seams, she stops with a tear-stained *Amen*. I can speak six languages: English—because my teacher whips anyone who doesn't speak it; Bemba—for my nanny, who has been with us since before my memory crystallized; French, which my mother teaches at the Girls Secondary School near the town fence; and enough Tonga, Nyanja, and Luvale for all the grown-ups who hear me to fawn and say *Wow, such a clever girl*. But what language does God speak, one of my six or one of these tongues? I wonder if mouthing along with my mother would count as my seventh, even though I can't entirely untangle the meaning from the sounds.

Whatever language God speaks, it is not one of these because my mother will come to this Bible study waiting for the restoration promise until I've outgrown her lap.

LOVE LETTERS FROM
MY FATHER'S DAUGHTER

I.

tell them i wish upon a time machine
press an exploding red button
leap into March of '57
the cusp of Britain relenting
my father's head
a tiny pulsing seed
the tail end of an unbearable urge
agape to everything
i discover him tender
soapy white foaming raw pink lips
dripping from his mother's fissured breasts
retrieve the steaming warmth
of this childhood nickname (Chinaka)
feathers in his siblings' cheeks
regarding a brand new baby brother
christening him something pliable (the gentle one)
before i came wearing fatherhood
to ruin him

II.

that//
under a microscope, i want to snatch the shape of the delicate mirage
of my father//as light as i was to the mid boys i let ravage me at
sixteen

    or//forgive.

        but//His face slivers like dust in December rain,
before inswa crawl
out of the cracks in our foundation

        & relief slips in the mud
with yellowed mangoes
delirious children calling Christmas

        i want to be as soft on his laughter ping-ponging in
a crevice of abandoned recollections as i was to friends who carried
stories about the crash site of my divorce into bonding sessions over
glasses of *Four Cousins*

or//forget

III.

that, on a ledge sometimes, i tug on the fibreglass of betrayals i've
seen since my father & mutate—eleven again, hands-to-head wailing
at the foot of his coffin, just like his sisters. my knees are jelly, should
tip me over, but instead, they glue me down to consider the splinters,
one by one, ignore the twitch in memory, a whispering, *Call Dad.*
Call Dad. Call Dad his number a ping-pong in my mind since '99
he will right the ashen stirring with those jokes of his—draw out my
laughter so big it spikes pain through my ribs.

breathe

or keep laughing
because
when i finally get the call—a *Yes*, sitting like a lady on the other end.
in that splice of time where i am brimming with choking joy, like too
much birthday cake frosting at my 7th birthday, i could forget, right?
everything.
could seize the ping-pong, tell him, *Yes*, he did his best & *See*
i still know how to make a smile of our features &

death didn't take everything
after all.

IV.

that

the trouble with healing
with my injury blurring into blemish
is that my father sheds his sharp lines
ceases to be just
The man who hit my mother
who punished us with starvation
who taught me how to flatten Hope
with words carefully arranged like a
flaming centipede
crawling across tongue
the trouble now
He shrinks into just a boy
ruptured as a sapling
me. him. we

trouble dislodges my rage
renders it homeless

MWANA

1. mwana escapes into the world
before the veins
which breed children
curdle. here, mothers are still
sacred caves.
babies are just babies.
rain not yet venomous

pain, searing open
sores into dewy skin.
this is the January of old
the sunrise here is ablaze
bleeding pigment into every body
the international news is still blaming the rising death
toll on gay men

even in this post-GRID age.
but no one is counting
women. infants.
the year is 1988
in a land carved to mirror a butterfly
mid-flight. by the insatiable
hands of 1964.

under the curfew/s
caged shops.
unfettered movement
but they cling still
to that God.
in his fair
& his justice

in the power
of frenzied little
prayers
in believing
Psalms 105: 15 in (Touch not mine anointed)
& Exodus 15:26 & (I am the Lord, who heals you)

2. mwana's sibling is delivered two
years belated. this iteration
of the womb
already hostile.
a once snug home
now a howling
devouring drum

this is May
& 1990 is a frigid quiet.
this sibling escaped
too fragile
for the hard mouth
of a bruised
world

the year is 1996
the nurses are jaded
the politicians are jaded
the journalists are jaded
the morticians are jaded
now all that

kangaroo care is rendered futile
the breastfeeding
futile
the education, tenderness
futile, futile
the measles vaccine
the hospital is futile

the doctor's pen, futile
her six years, futile
that final fraction of a smile
on the budding face,
futile. the mauve box holding

the body too small, futile
the funeral wailing,
the little iridescent dress,
the demise itself, fucking futile

3. mwana stands over a rusting
spade of just turned
April ground
in her ten-year-old
fingers
ground sours
that instant, a favorite season

tilts,
no longer a fulfilled promise
of sheets of rain
knocking against locked windows
or soft guavas landing
split
mwana's mother bringing in

a withering
smile, a tray of steaming sweet potatoes
sugared, milked tea
waiting for inswa
in the pre-morning
collected in flaking metal bowls
from disintegrating corners

of houses to be sizzled later
over a fire
snacked on. that taste—
galaxies better than popped corn.
but still joy wilts,
Dust to dust, the preacher calls it
Ashes to ashes, as mwana tosses it

mangles itself inside her
nostrils now
the aroma of starved earth,
the brilliant white
of a mother's new coffinment
waiting to receive it,
a pumpkin seed that now will never sprout.

4. mwana returns a final time
sardined by the broad-leaved
shepherds-trees & the blistered stones
on hardened sand
two decades between
the first & this
but her dance is from memory.

to falter past the box,
to pause at the glass
to attempt recognition at this
sunken

face
to free a river of tears
to welcome faceless hugs

mwana's mind has stalked
this terrain in dreams
until they've insisted on her
presence.
when parents call a mwana, she must answer
Mukwai? with her mother's
voice and the slits her father lent her

for a mouth.
Exodus 20:12 (Honor your father and your mother,
that you may have a long life) demand
ancestors intonations
raw
mwana has waited too long
the soil is already
belching weeds.

this excavation is futile
mwana will never find the
sistermotherfather.
a laugh slams itself into her chest,
raptures
convoluted
a whimper

PROTO

On your mother's lap,
see how your view is glorious.
trace wrinkles of joy cupping her smile,
catch laughter supplanting fatigue, how it pinches her eyes.

Say *Mama.*

You will not.
Eight months old.
your knees
are still your feet

the truant thing, an outsider
noosed into you
like a plait weaved
from eternal dreadlocks

to unwind it
you must sever yourself.
On this morning, you abandon
weeping for speech
there's a flurry—

scampering
to grab a phone,
steadying
a quivering hand to capture–

Ta-ta.

Tighter.

Tata.

your introductory lesson
in pretending
that the grin receiving you-
r first word

wasn't once
upon your vessel.
Of forgetting the bite
marks you imprinted

on her nipples.
Unknowing that the day
you bled from her like puss
from chilonda,

she parted with herself.
Re-christened *Mother*
hyphenated with you
but oh, the recklessness of children

a baby's—*Tata*
a toddler's—*Ba Tata*
teenagers'—*My Father*
when the earth

ly ones shatter
their hearts
Our Father.
tears ousted

by clasped hands
staring at a galvanized roof
imagining beyond it
& the bricks

holding it down
& the tree
shading it
from nature.

Tata

in the heavens.
the truant thing,
an invisible deity who holds
your mother's conscience hostage.

At the burial —*Mayo! Why have you forsaken me?*

OUR FATHER

: our father, eavesdropping
on the mattress. is there a telephone
cord between Mayo's clasped fingers?
does it lift the tendrils of her strangled whispers
all the way up to your alabaster castle?
is Gabrīēlle an irate switchboard operator
with a rouged mouth & glasses zooming in on bloodshot eyes?
the glitch in Jesus' refilling our mealie meal container

i carry an empty metal bowl, knock on our neighbor's
kitchen door where *Please* sits with *may we borrow* & my wrinkled
shame as i curtsy a *Thank you*
maybe God is still busy.
maybe Mayo is still on hold.
maybe us singing, *Jehovah Jireh, mwimbileni!* is the on-hold music
maybe her payphone tokens ran out before we said
In Jesus' mighty name, Amen.

UBUTATA, KUTATISHYANYA

After YANYI

Four ghosts at this table,
three living, one me.

I am asleep, & there I am dying.
The last thing that I remember will un–
ravel itself in the nightmare. The beast
will return me: my whole life spooled out
of his mouth, the backwards words of him unloving me.
There stands my Father who is also the
grave digger. In the nightmare, does it
matter that he never wanted me? In
the nightmare, when he talks, my blood is black & then clear,
& he leads me to the head shaped hole where
I can reach him & then he leaves. On cue
the owls will soon want nothing but to mourn
for him. & on cue the jacarandas blaze purple & then
fall, this father unmaking love from me & scattering
my pieces everywhere, I'll go. Until the end.
Then he is the language, too. Backwards words woven into
the nightmare as it began to happen.

TATA

Recipe

Served close to the sky, with a hot, gruff beard, after boiling for thirty years in a bubbling temper, this father is comfort as you will know it best.

Rate this recipe:

- 3 Stars from 2 votes
- Prep Time: 40 weeks
- Cook Time: 30 years
- Additional Time: 11 years, 7 months
- Total Time: Approx. 42 years

Serves 0

PHOTOGRAPH RECIPE
FRAME RECIPE

PARENT/HUMAN - <u>jump to recipe</u>

This is ~~not~~ an old family concoction. My ancestors ~~didn't~~ smuggle it from grip to grip like a generation conversing with the next in a code of inextinguishable fire. This ingredient list was ~~not~~ folded until it could hide in the tied corner at a Grandmother's chitenge 1500 years ago as she threaded the Congo rain forests to exhale Mbemba Nshinga. The measurements were not tried and then girdled like a secret to the chests of my people as they swelled across Rhodesia, Nzambi Enzi, Zambia. These are scraps of memories convened behind an eleven-year-old's eyes, tracking the frenzied last movements of a wounded father and the languid reactions of the living. For this recipe, you will need just six simple ingredients:

Ingredients

+ **Peter Stuyvesant Cigarettes**—To dim Aramis with the whiff of nicotine puffed in singles on Sundays, nursing a hangover with a moist face cloth on the sofa.

+ **Tracy Chapman**—On Vinyl LPs, not cassette tape, to distill the guitar chords in the commotion of Lui Road.

+ **A ragged voice**—To ferment place next to tenderness in the dictionary of memory.

+ **A greying goatee**

+ **Blue jeans**—Ironed.

+ **Crisp cotton shirts**—Tucked in to veil the rumpled edges of the person and douse in regret later.

Instructions

1. Wipe out his ashtrays

2. Place glass where his arms can stretch and locate them before anger shakes his fingers, rearranges them into fists, and finds a face in which to free them.

Next to his recliner in the sitting room is best but for good measure. place another under the lemon tree in front of the veranda another with the empty Mosi bottles in the kitchen another on his bedside table and just to be sure, next to the blown-up black and white iteration of your mother in her youngest years with her blown-out Afro rounding her cheeks.

3. Watch the trays refill with ash, see it float into the air, mingle with your voice brumming *Don't you know you better run, run, run, run, run, run Run, run, run, run, run, run* before landing on your mother's buffed floors.

4. Take the Kwacha notes he hands you and desert the shouting inside the walls of the house, find the kantemba to buy him more.

Keep the change, baby girl: a prayer and a promise.

5. Master the way his mouth slackens when *Why?* plays. Aim for the lyrics in the quiet after of his explosion.

Why is a woman still not safe, when she's in her home?

6. Knead it inside your throat, form an echo until your voice wears the same frayed notes as his.

7. Nuzzle into his beard, the bobbing rock in his neck, and the Sta-soft lavender of the cotton shirt your mother starched for him that morning.

8. Serve warm, like an iron to denim, whenever the memory strays time.

ANKYLOGLOSSIA

in this life cycle/ Mother
Tongue is an untamed garden/

your lips/ its lax wardens/
mouth/ a country

brimming with your once
enslaved clansmen/

weeds of other dialects
sprout convoluted/

formerly living organs/
vowelsconsonantssyllables/

wiped out in a wrestling ring
camouflaged as school/

tender footed voices
haemorrhaging nursery rhymes

ABCDEF*u*G*ee*
urged by the blunt backs

of dusters
against fingerpads/

stripped mulberry sticks
whipping palms/

in this life cycle/that dazed
gash/ your face/

carries the recollections of all itselves/
the next time you race

out of your father/
when the yolk of your final

mother accepts you/
feel for the missing

tether at the floor
of your mouth/

do not conflate
the razor's scar for *emancipation.*

HOMEGOING

4.

before abandoning my fatherland/ i must first dignify this
departure with marble & granite/

bribe someone to chip *Here lies a beloved* beneath the carving of an
angel etched above April 14th

1958—July 28th 1999. but of course/ Lusaka City Council has lost
his plot/on the old Leopards' Hill / i have to bribe somebody and
then another somebody to retrieve

the tattered death registry/ leaf pages/ walk backwards/

Of course, I remember the date i tell the third somebody

3.

i must first eulogize 20 years too late

locate K & scroll/ *should i use his english name*

before his Bemba one/*Fuck you* to his mantra/bitter laugh dance
in my gut/

an African must not bear a white man's name. i can't find him/
Damnit Dad/

2.

KA/KAB/KAC/KAL/

a fourth somebody is pacing/*How far madam?* squeezing Lusaka
humidity with *are you sure about the date?*

fyola, but not loud enough for this somebody to hear my teeth kiss.
i'm sure/about all the exhausted wailing when i walked into the
funeral house/ of

Maama's breath hitching/*God. You look just like your father*—just
yesterday was her baby. i'm sure about the cortège of deaths smirk
inside the hearse/i'm sure of the fresh wounds in the

earth & flame trees bowing around winding dirt paths/

still/*I can't find him.*

1.

not without a mirror to say/

There is our nose daughter

the birthmark we share on our philtrum.

There, lips lined black from his smoking, racing through my mother
to darken mine too.

There is the dark behind our eyes, which splinters every time we laugh.

MWANA WANCHETE EMVWELA KHUMPELO

here is my village
(Mukanga)[1]

           the Father who built[2] me
        the sister (not mine) who unkept[3] me,

    here, my revolving door of teachers[4]

            the   classrooms

            brimming

              here, the friends

            who held me

TLC—chasing waterfalls—beats to hide in

            here, Psalm 68:5[5] and the
        God who never came

.

---

1   but read Thornpark & Chilulu & Kamwala & that one neighbourhood behind the warehouses
2   lent me an X and then fled
3   a child needs more than a roof and a quiet stomach to be smothered/mothered
4   switching primary schools like underwear
5   Father to the fatherless?

here, the Colossians 3:18[6] marriage that failed to dissolve me

here lamentations

before the birthings

finally love[7]

---

6   Wives, submit to your husbands, as is fitting in the Lord.

7   here i am, unburied

PART II

ANOTHER MOTHER DOES NOT COME WHEN YOURS DIES II

I learn how to pray the last week of school. That morning, when the school security guard unlocks the building and sunlight floods the narrow corridor, we are greeted by rolls of pink and green tissue stuck to the ceiling with Sellotape. Between the headmistress' office and the girls' toilet, a wooden chair has been placed on a podium and the tissue paper there has been fashioned into the shape of open flowers, like the ones we draw when the assignment is to make Mother's Day cards.

Father Christmas aleisa, Mwape, the class bully, squeals. Teacher Harriet knocks him on the head for propping one Bemba word against the two English ones, and for the rest of the day, he takes it upon himself to do the same to any other transgressor he hears. Usually, I know what my classmates are curious about and pride myself in explaining it to them. Important things like *The Lady in the TV advert isn't really called Miss Zambia, she is just the prettiest, so they let her use the whole country's name*, and *Yes, you can make Coca-Cola with tea leaves, you just have to be careful to strain out the gunk, cool it and put ice in it before drinking*, and *Buttercup and Margarine are sometimes the same thing, but only if your mum knows to buy it from Mwaiseni and not the nearest kantemba, which doesn't even have a fridge*. Everyone usually believes me on account of me being the only one who hadn't gone mute on the first day when Teacher Harriet said, *Don't speak Bemba, speak English*, as she stalked the spaces between our desks while brandishing her long wooden ruler. But this, *Father Christmas*, is as new as leather school shoes from Bata. So, though I nod with the rest of my classmates at Mwape's pronouncement, pretending to be just as jittery with glee, I hope no one asks me before I can come up with a believable definition for who exactly Father Christmas is.

Fortunately, they are all soon too busy playing *What Will Father Christmas Bring Me?* to bombard me with any stupid questions. There is talk of *Shera*-shaped dolls and those poofy organza dresses that the lucky girls who play flower girl get to wear. I mostly scowl at their guesses while thinking my hardest about what this *father* will bring that the other one hadn't.

On our last phone call, in the secretary's office at the school where my mother teaches, I asked my father for the entire Samantha Series. The one I had, *Samantha Learns a Lesson*, had taken me a whole month to finish. I figured by the time I finished the last one, I would have already forgotten the first and would still need to linger on the pages and ask my mother to sound out a long word for me.

Of course, baby, my father said, his silky voice crackling through the line like the TV when we turned it on during a storm. The call had come during guava season, and I had spent it using my tongue as a toothpick for the seeds stuck in the crevices of my teeth. It is deep into mango season now; none of us bother to steal some from the roadside stalls when the marketeers aren't looking. Our own mangoes have ripened into the colour of yolk, are falling from our backyard trees, rotting with the leaves. My mother packs one for me every day, calls it

Sweet Course because she cuts it into cubes first instead of letting me suck it off the seed and make a mess of my school clothes. Now, I try to squeeze the image of my father, already dimming into this Father Christmas, who apparently grants secret wishes like Cinderella's fairy godmother or my mother's God. I wonder if Father Christmas' voice breaks between words, even though he will be right in front of me on the wooden chair covered with tissues and not in a dorm room at a foreign University studying for his master's degree. I decide that if it doesn't, if, when Father Christmas talks, the sentences form straight lines from his mouth to my ears, then he can be trusted to deliver before the next guava season arrives. It's just a few thoughts, a few *Focus*, taps from Teacher Harriet throughout the day, but they hold me over somehow, dragging me from morning till the last bell.

Single file, order, single file! Teacher Harriet strains over the din of excitement that has gripped us. Bemba words are scampering from so many mouths at once, nobody caring now about the *Speak English* rule. The upcoming holidays are four weeks along, and day one started as soon as the bell sounded. Her rules didn't matter there. Eventually, she shrugs and frees us. We shuffle out into the corridor to join the other classes of pupils waiting to meet Father Christmas.

We are last in line, so Father Christmas' face is shielded by all the teachers standing with their classes upfront. Slowly, though, the corridor empties of bodies and that after-school oniony smell. Excited giggles filter in from outside as pupils unwrap presents. I find a tall window to peek through. I eye a boy hugging a stuffed animal shaped like a rabbit, and his friend talking to a skinny blonde doll wearing a pink sequin dress. Another boy is belching next to his blue car with blinking eyes where the headlights should be, and another is stuffing a short wooden train into his backpack. Someone received a plastic telephone and is inserting her index into the finger hole, rotating the dial clockwise. *Hello, hello,* she is saying. *Hello, may I help you?* before guffawing and startling a bird that had been pecking on a flower in the flame tree, which sits at the mouth of the schoolyard. Sometime between the bird flying off and the girl with the telephone disappearing into the street beyond the gate, *Hello,* becomes *Ho,* and then *Ho, ho, ho.*

Your turn, Teacher Harriet says with a hand on my shoulder, the plump fingers strong and the purple nails digging slightly into the fabric of my blouse.

Oh, I scream-say, the excitement squirrelling out through my mouth like a surprise burp.

I step forward to see a man as pale as baobab seeds before you suck the sweet off. He has on a red suit, and a stiff white wig hangs crookedly around his mouth.

Ho, ho, ho, he bellows again. *Come on.* Father Christmas sounds a little like the TV shows my mother watches at night. The ones I'm not supposed to be watching but have found a hole at the bottom of my bedroom door that lets me watch every single one. His skin is exactly like theirs, and his eyes are the same colour as my grandma's cats. I was going to tell him that I wanted a bicycle, that's what I decided while waiting to meet him, but I break out in hives, blinking at the cat eyes and the white wig and the baobab-pale skin and cry like I did on the first day of school. I run out of the building without collecting my bookbag. I was going to ask for a red bike with a basket at the front for me to put my bookbag in on the ride to school. I was going to ride it home and sound the horn at everyone on my path. Now—

I tell my mother half the story between sobs. About a scary man and *Ho, ho, ho* and the bike I wanted for Christmas.

Christmas? She says, making a face like she smells liver cooking.

Christmas? I echo, doubting myself.

Well, we don't do Christmas around here, okay? That's not even Jesus' birthday.

When is Jesus' birthday? I ask, welling up again, thinking about my almost bike.

Aw, she says, pulling me to her, where her voice thrumming in her chest can soothe me. She smells a little like the carbolic soap sitting on a plastic tray in the bathroom, a little like the vegetable oil she uses on her skin when lotion runs out before the month end, a little like me.

The bicycle was going to have a bell, and sparkles on the handlebar, I muffle into her blouse, saliva, and mucus, wetting it and sticking to her skin.

She stiffens slightly but says, *Well, if you want a bicycle, baby, you can pray for one. Our Father in Heaven will provide.*

I can't explain it, but that makes me sob even harder, like the time she picked Sprite instead of Fanta at the takeaway, and I hated that she would have to experience the fizz shooting through her nose after every swallow like I had the one time I had tried the horrid drink.

Trust me, baby, my mother says, raking my hair. *Our Father in Heaven always answers.* My mother's mantra: when the school sent me away for one term because she couldn't pay the fees; when her salary was delayed three weeks and we ran out of food, even mealie meal to make porridge in the morning; even when we slept through thieves breaking into our house and taking everything but the bed and mosquito net we shared.

How would our Father in Heaven answer when I didn't even speak his language?

The crying has me depleted, and I choose instead to trust the memory of every truth my mother has ever shared. So that night, I pray the way my mother does, quiet and soft, *Amen*-ing and *Amen*-ing and then right before we were due to finish, I convulse into a litany of senseless drivel, again and again, and again. My mother is staring at me when I open my eyes, she says nothing.

POKUFWA LINI ANYOKO POWELA MUYAKINÉ

So, memorise the rushing web of blood vessels
lining your mother's womb.

Greet the almost kin buried there.
Tattoo the shape of the grave she carved in herself to grow you.
Record her first scream.
Play it on a loop.

Call it *I love you.*

Bottle the taste of her life dripping on your tongue.
Wrap yourself around her chest.
Grab every chord on Earth.
Turn it into the praise songs you hum into her breast.

Shout her name until your voice is gravel.

Watch her ghost reply.
Steal the sound of its laughter bubbling up her seared throat.
Call it resemblance.
Listen to the drum in her chest.

Search for it forever in music.
You will never find it.

MAYOSENGÉ

because, the word *Auntie* is non-existent in Bemba.
in its almost   place,

the second sister   so,
or/phan should be a

butchered abomination
& because there is an overabundance of milk duct orifices

to latch/
To wean

for malnutrition.
these sisters wear the same sanpaku.

i should locate myself
in them

on my mother/s last bed
a sister should stand

clasp my hand, repossess
the shape of a mother's endearments

my feet burn
my shape into the ground

til the ivies
surrender

again.
again

MAYO MPAPA NAINÉ NKAKUPAPA—

this is a wisdom for wombs

who won't trail the slick scent of their daughter's cadavers,
tongues who can afford,
the flavour of arrogance,

this is how you fold yourself, daughter
strap a body to your back
sing *auwe—ash baby—*sleep baby
—dream of elation before you forget
     sweet salt leaking from your mother's breasts
      her breath a hot warning

call it,
wisdom

mother, carry me on your back
one day I will carry you too
a promise not for the lap
whose load won't allow
life long enough
for daughters to fill out their bodies
     mouths to sing

—mother, carry me on your back
and one day I will carry you too

ANYOKO NANYOKO MPHELA

daddy has smuggled me into a
cubicle
calling it your room

the air in here is bleach,
& medicine.

wilting roses from the last time he
pummelled
you sit in the vase on the window
sill

the aunties are here, cramming
rapid
sentences into this tiny airless room

like terrified children
caught stealing nyama from the pot

there is a ghost in your bed
wearing your translucent lavender
nightdress

she blinks slow, like you, but
whispers my name in spurts
each syllable snapped from the next

like an unpractised mouth
as she pries her lips apart

yellowing teeth and spit bubbles
marking each corner

she says, *Come*
in a thunderless voice

but she isn't you, Mum, is she?
not that parched mouth

begging
Please, baby, don't cry.

those limp arms yawning
Give me a hug.

the crater pretending to be
your chest, or the bleak stench
which has

supplanted cocoa butter and Bu-
tone on your skin

not that whining voice
Please, leka ukulila

KATONTHO KOLILA M'TEMBO.

Proverbs 31.
Stiff flesh nourishing
weeds.
Rest the
wife ground to powder.
Her man, a pestle.

Her last bed becomes the snake's veranda,
indecipherable lines winding into the earth's core.
Here lies a moon trained to flicker,
sugarcane that never became
Mazabuka sweet
or blind, blind joy.

Skin of bones—
ablactated on enduring, jagged affection split
among ten thousand others. Here lies
a body stitched from raptured
promises misnamed
Hope.

Her bound-up laughter flung
everywhere. Left-over drumming long
after the secret lessons ended, congealed
bodies, soothingfastingpraying.
Here is shame sprouting like
hair between thighs.

A fist clenched tight
between teeth, rotting mid-
chew. Here is
Woman,
next to
Single mother
in Malachi 2:16.

Her snapped bones,
tears gather too late under the
funeral tent. Rest easy ~~single~~
mother. Lump in the soil rusted
taste of metal
erasing you

"MWIMBONA AMAMBA MUNUMA"

(© 1988 Bana Me's singing drums of laughter rolling off Bina Hope
this tune is Bina Laika's wisdom brewed over an ancient flame
a refrain of dancing ululations swaying from the women who once housed me)

Mwimbona amamba munuma (x2)

what if those scales burnt into my mother's
back were remnants of every time she strapped me
into her chitenge, swallowed her sobs
to save me from knowing the shape of fists

Niné na fyala uyu mwana, niné na fyala iyi mbeka

If I'm the winged star she birthed, would she chant
"You were worth it" (You are worth it. You are worth it. You are)
would the chorus form the constellations,
which sank with her in that crisp white casket?

Tiny bones
litter
the cemetery floor,
thorns where her spine should be

Nine na fyala iyi mbeka

CHAONA MUYAKO CHASILA, MAILO CHILI PAKO

When my uncle's wife asks me if now that I have a baby
I'm finally over my Mother
like Mother is synonymous with hurdle
the screech I choke on is

Listen, you cocky little bitch

that green mourning tent
is still pitched like a chitambala on my head
even after fifteen fucking years.

I am wounded earth
hands raging above my head
I am my grandmother's howl,

shards of wrecked silence blinding
wet fear, uneven chitenge wrapped around
my little girl legs ageing into my mother's shames.

My uncle's wife smiles,
and I remember myself,
a Zambian girl raised on affability
and I-should-have-saids

out loud
I say

Nothing.

now this belated
hate mail is a mangled
whisper into a steaming shower,

you think you'll never learn how to bandage
your own oozing fontanel, enh?
                    wait.

DREAM

i am ten going on thirty-six when my mother holds me like a petal and

considers her creation. her Afro is strangled in a puff, the grey highlights

winking in the sun. she is thirty-three going on sixty and it's warm here,

a sun i used to know. she kisses me on the cheek, plants a disappearing

red stain which I try to coax with one cupped palm—*Stay, Stay.*

I love you—she says. a plume of breath. *I am so proud,* a half-whisper

Thank you—I want to tell her, and—*Where the hell have you been?*

but my alarm springs to life, the phone screen an insistent blue

& spirit descends into body again

the room stiff and whole again

here, she is

forever thirty-three

PART III

ANOTHER MOTHER DOES NOT COME WHEN YOURS DIES   III

Prayer floats back into my mouth two years after my father returns and we play house again even though at night, he fights my mother until she escapes to my room, sobbing while I feign sleep.

I am ten and have four and a half languages left on my tongue: English, which my father calls the queen's language when he's drunk and only wants to watch the BBC; Nyanja, because that's what all my schoolmates speak and they won't play with a chongololo who thinks she is *up there* with her English manners; Bemba, which my father insists on when he grows taciturn, Our *language is our identity*, he says; Tonga, because despite his belligerence when someone is disparaging the language in public, he is afraid of my mother's mother, and doesn't want to explain why I lost that part of my tongue after living with him only two and a half years. The half is the sporadic French I've retained in my mother's most frequented instructions, like *Arrêt* and *Ferme la porte* and *Silence*, which her friends still fawn over because I have the accent just right from hearing her since I was little. In church on Sunday, when the pastor commands the congregation to *Speak to the Lord your God from the heart*, my mother still breaks into tongues with the rest of them. I can watch because their eyes are squeezed shut. I watch her each time like it is the first, trying to make meaning of her tear-stained plea, the one she is still waiting on God to answer.

One day my mother says, *Pray for me; I have a cold*, which isn't true, even though she is staying home from work and hasn't opened the curtains or windows in her bedroom. Sunlight still creeps in through tiny gaps the curtains fail to conceal, revealing the inky stain on her cheek and cut across her lip from their last altercation. But I pray.

A few days later, when she returns from a *check-up* at the hospital, my mother coughs and says, *Pray for me, baby, the doctors say ni TB.*

Later that week, my prayer is needed again, this time *so that the medicine will work.*

And then a month later? Maybe several, *Pray* trails off in her mouth. Her voice seems to fight her, and she coughs with the same might as my father after half a pack of Peter Stuyvesants. The single word contorts her face while the rest of her body lies flat on a tall, white hospital bed. It is not new, this praying away of sickness. The first time my mother had TB, it took many injections and as many prayers for her to stop lying on her chest because her bottom was sore and start going to work again. The second time was shorter, but the coughing was worse. At the tail end of every other bout of illness, every other prayer, she had convalesced, and I had returned to fighting her— refusing to wash the plates after lunch, staying out too late on the road with my friends, playing waida.

This third time isn't bending to the *Our Father* I can now recite. Every time she seems to get better, her body shifts shape, dips for the worse. I have grown afraid of the cracking in her voice; I hope it won't disappear completely, like the fat around her face and tiny patches of hair at her temples, so I pray. I pray the way she does, on my knees, begging in a language I still don't understand. I don't mind that the aunties are staring, that the beeping is probably drowning my voice out in God's ear, or even that my mother is rubbing my back gently, sobbing. God is quiet, watching me unspool from the centre out.

The pastor prays over her, promises restoration and everyone but me says, *Amen.*

MATRIPHAGY

webbed venter served on your breakfast plate
all simmering/rotten promises
she whisked for herself
at sixteen/staring at this gaping oyster

for lunch/conspire with her body's rebellion
expel you wet with muck
& blood
& a thousand unrecognisable hunks of her

Hello little moon/
she will say
before the door tears
& love metastasises

*Hello/*you might say/
if the words were not disfigured/
forgotten tendrils
from the world before

here/for lunch/a critics eye on the   spoor carved path
          & harried lessons in her grandmother's tongue
while the schools beat it out with the back end of dusters & plant
in its stead this   one/ by which you are now bound

This is how you cook nsima/she might be saying/
if the smoke/the fire/the steam/
angry water gulping handfuls
of mealie meal would relent and make room for her voice

for supper/a boil
fresh as the time she said *No* a hundredth time & you finally spat back
the ball of herself she became
beneath the weight of expectation

VOW

Chapter 1

"Where you go I will go, and where you stay I will stay. Your people
will be my people and your God my God. Where you die I will
die, and there I will be buried."

1: Like this, I took a stranger, roped in the law and called him Husband.
Like this, I had and held from a dusty August day for better and for
worse, for richer and for poorer, in sickness and in health, until death
knocked, cradled our chins, made eye contact and asked if we would
kiss him. Like that, I loved and honoured until I was bled dry of life.

2: I have known you for eight of my twenty-eight years; have
embraced you nearly all of them and meant it when I mimicked
Ruth in the chapel even though my voice was unsure of itself I went
everywhere you went—remember how we walked twenty k's from
school and back because our salaries hadn't made it to the end of
the month again and we didn't have enough for the bus fare? and
stayed—remember our first flat, with the holes in the roof that
told us when to wake up because the sun cut through the tiles onto
our sleep? Your people—because I was a stray—became mine—it
was so easy, too; what with our God being the same guy — our
harmonies in Sabbath school, but yesterday, when you snuck your
tablets of crack into our two-year-old's backpack, knowing in his
eyes the rocks would be white sweets, that he'd swallow them
without chewing the way he did every other treat, that it would

shoot straight to his brain and destroy what we had foolishly
created, the one we almost named after our near love, that's when I
knew I would not die where you did.

3: & like that, March came, evidence was considered, I became a
Petitioner, you a Respondent, a declaration was made, your behaviour
unreasonable, I did the proving and the vows were untied, irretrievably
broken down dissolved, absolute.

MY MOTHER'S FAVOURITE FOOD

but first
my father's favourite
was fish & chips
a taste acquired in the two years he called

Cardiff, home/
fattening his engineering degree.
the potatoes had to be sliced into circles
crisped using my mother's four-step process

> /soak the starch out/
> /parboil/
> /pat dry/
> /double fry/

he liked it for breakfast
recovering from those nights he came home angry/
his fists greeting
my mother's body

he liked it sprinkled
red with crushed chilis
red where his hands had left lacerations
where my mother leaked like a heavy cloud.

eating the sun with her skin/
singing into the fire
my mother recreated this favourite
best at fighting the grog in his voice

                                        the morning after
                                              we bury
                                           my mother
                                    he wakes up ravenous

                                     /he takes his seat/
                                     /unfolds his fists/
                                     /cradles his face/
                                           weeps.

& I never knew my mother's favourite food

PART IV

ANOTHER MOTHER DOES NOT COME WHEN YOURS DIES IV

The second Wednesday in April, I come home to an army green tent perched on my father's pristine lawn. The sitting room chairs are arranged in a semi-circle to honour a hissing fire. My grandmother arrives right after me, screaming my mother's name. Yet the morning after, I still wake up expecting my mother to come into my room and tell me to get ready for school.

After four days of wail-drenched air, I take the silent car ride to the cemetery. Through the window, Lusaka peels by. The sun is in the sky's belly button, reducing the buzzing city to a silhouette, from the high-rise flats in Kabwata to the rolling mansions lining Leopards Hill road.

In the Mourner's Shelter, I stand in a line next to my father, watching person after person approach a gleaming white coffin and disintegrate at the head. My turn comes too soon, before I can decide whether I am ready. My feet stiffen at the fishtail, the world spinning out of shape. My father, who has been sobbing non-stop, wipes snot with the sleeve of his plaid, patch-work jacket, and offers his hand so that we can walk to the front together. It is so tender, my father's hand—bordering on fragile. Even without touching it now, I know it to be as supple as just-fried tilapia, like it couldn't bruise a fly, let alone a mother, let alone mine. After their brawls, these hands would soothe my mother. A moth on her forehead and cheeks, as soft as him calling her *my love* asking *how are you feeling today?*

Come, baby, he says to me, voice crinkled from the weeping, breath laced with cigarette smoke.

The stiffness in my legs zips to my mouth, grits my teeth until the rhythm of my heart threatens to rip them, one by one, from my gums. I proceed anyway, walking in my father's steps like an echo. Nobody has said, *Banoko naba fwa,* so there is hope. Yes, I am scaling the edge of the white casket, taking my time to get to the glass window where everyone before me has been stopping, some reaching their hands in to caress. Yes, my stupid heart starts to rage, my ears churning out a whine. Yes, I know the mourners are shouting her name, hands cradling heads and pitying me with their eyes, but still—

As I reach the little window, I suddenly remember that I don't know where I put my photo album, the one with all the pictures my mother and I took at *Phoenix Photo Studio*—a panic courses through me, hot and crippling. I hold the edge of the white box and photograph her with my eyes. One of the wailers screams my name and scolds my mother for leaving.

Mum has on a lilac suit with flappy peach collars, silver studs, red lipstick, and a small loose fringe made with the curls from her last relaxer. She is wearing that concentration face of hers that cuts the width of her lips in half. Her face is sunken, lustre sucked from it like air from a popped balloon, nothing like all the times before.

Mummy, I whisper like I do when she is napping, and I want to ask her for something.

Mummy, please! A scream.

In slumber, my mother's eyelids flutter, the whites of her eyes partially visible. Now they are stubbornly shut. In the end, it's the way she doesn't smile. The way her arms don't reach for me, or her voice still groggy, saying *Why are you watching me sleeping?* That's how I know. That is how I know my mother is dead.

*

The next day, I move to my mother's sister's house—step one of my father melting into the fringes before Death returns for a refill, fifteen months later.

My mother's sister's house is twice the size of ours, nestled in a plush neighbourhood lined by bushwillow trees, fresh brick fences, and tall, burnished gates. The inside smells like a mix of garlic sizzling in oil and a perfume I cannot name. My first meal there is char-grilled pork chops on a bed of white rice and red sauce. At my mother's house, rice was reserved for birthdays or my father's lightened mood. I scoop the rice and sweep the pork from one side of the plate to the other until my wrist grows numb. Afterwards, the sister—who has my mother's eyes, has the same even dark complexion and sprinkling of skin tags across her cheeks—asks me why I didn't touch my ndiyo. I am not a quiet child. Any other day I would have simply said, *I don't like it.* I would have wrinkled my nose and shivered at the mere idea of the fat cooling from the pork and beading on my tongue. But I haven't stopped thinking of my sleeping mother, of her skewed rouge and that delicate suit. I don't want to say anything new, don't want fresh snapshots to take up space in my mind lest I forget, so instead, I start to cry.

My mother's sister cocks her head to the side, the way my mother ~~does~~, did. Only it's the left side, not the right. She tells me to wash my plate and all the dirty dishes, she doesn't like lazy girls. I nod, even as the tears continue into the kitchen, over the sink, and then the bedroom afterwards until sleep comes.

I dream of my mother laughing. It is the shade of a Bhutan Glory butterfly.

ISHINA

practice my contours inside your private time
with your looking glass

My father taught me how to sit
still, when someone
misdirects their tongue on the u,
sharpens a b
already
cooked perfect
in   the porridge of softness,
of our mother tongue
or deciding midway not to travel
all
se
ven
syllables
of us.

practice the tree
our woodsmen could not
conquer

                                                                still

VERTIGO

Or my mother, 23 and bursting at the seams with hope. She is a daughter of independence, bled from her mother in the blur that is Nzambi enzi, Rhodesia and Zambia. There is my father, filled with the arrogance of the freshly educated in a time when not many like him are. Together, they trade words in the language which university tables have woven into them. They spill laughter and scatter birds from rooftops. My mother, 23 and foolish, misnames the flutters which swell in her gut "love". My father, 29 and broken, flees the weight of this responsibility. The doctor scribbles Gravindex one on scrap paper, and just like that, at the tail end of January on a Friday drenched in rain, 1988, a daughter, bursting at the seams with dreams, is born. She is a daughter of Hope, bled from her mother in the blur that is the GRID age, multi-party democracy and Zambia.

& then there I am, filled with the arrogance of the freshly educated. I think I know better, now that I am fluent in the language which university tables have woven into me. When I spill my laughter onto Chachacha, I let it float with dust devils, across the blistered tar and listen to its echo expand between the buildings as fat as all my most foolish dreams. I am 24 and I know better, even as I misname the flutters which swell in my gut "love"—as the man I marry shrinks in the face of this new responsibility. Gravindex one, say the doctors, and just like that, on the tail end of April, a brittle Monday, 2013, a boy is born. And I, drunk with the madness of birthing and loving and terror, dare to hope, *together, may we trick fate.*

KU CHALO

when a Bemba girl trades her homeland for a Delta aircraft, she doesn't
know what this virgin voyage will steal. it mirrors her most recent
birthday all—sleeplessness & excitement bubbling with supper like
mush on the verge of becoming
nshima.

when a Bemba girl scuttles from dim terminal, across the hot tarmac,
to the gleaming staircase, she leaves more than the oppressive October
Sun and August dust
at the yawning door
the air inside rebirths itself, sixteenth birthday crisp.

Atlanta lights incite her fevered heartbeat
her Zambian accent is already bending itself
when the Bemba girl says *I'm here to study* at Customs, her voice crawls
into her chest and withers with the chill in the air.

through the rivers whispering along her fingertips,
the biometrics machine sucks into itself the Bemba girl's disdain
for the oil stains left by Maama's vitumbuwa, & viwaya wedged in a
molar cavity with the puffed-out corn & the slick sweetness of zigolo,
which raised her.

when another professor twists the consonants of the Bemba girl's name,
something snaps the contours of ZESCO power cuts,
morphs blacked-out weekends into her nieces and nephews laughing
in Independence Day showers.

those year-long Lusaka potholes ram themselves into
the same crannies of the Bemba girl's mind where mango pulp
slithers down her fingers, they become that first bite of Christmas
chicken,
become Mayo's hands slicking Vaseline down her face.

as if, without the sun beating her up at a School assembly *Stand and
Sing of Zambia* is drained of power to deplete *Proud and Free* is a
shouted refrain in her head even if the vowels, they have died panono,
panono each time she's had to say Uhm—actually it's Mubanga, not,
Mugamba?

MUSHOBO

not your mother tongue, but i might be peanut butter sticky to
roof of your half-open mouth and take up residence there. not your
daddy's child, you might confuse me for the monsters you cook
inside your closet walls mid-dream. not you, but might find me
metastatic, leaping back from the echo of my eyes.
                                                            afraid
                                                        i'll bite.
                                    clog your arteries with
                                    delirium

TUCKED IN

My son watches Bambi for the first time today. An hour and ten minutes of decadent silence—no banging toys, no merry-go-rounds of questions and requests. I welcome this quiet for the gift that it is: rare solitude for my mind.

After, his afternoon continues as always—Legos, Pokémon, Beyblade, a loud, imaginary world that turns the house upside down, until supper.

Then, as I bend over to tuck him in at bedtime, he says, "Mom, I have a question."

I smile. "Oh?" Usually, his questions just spill out, no preamble or room to answer before the next one comes, for as long as he can stave off my inevitable *Goodnight*. I tap his nose with my finger. "And what's that question?"

"Will you die?"

He is eight. So far, our big talk has been about why daily showers are important, even when he doesn't get any mulch in his socks. I was expecting *the birds and the bees* before the *life-and-death* conversation. My heart metamorphosises to fissure as I tell him, "One day, yes, I will die."

The silence returns, the one from Bambi, no longer a gift, as my mind tries to squirrel away from his inquisitiveness. His eyes, which were once my mother's eyes, dark and wide, seem to take a long screenshot of my face, memorising the routes of the lines on my skin as the understanding sinks into him. The silence blooms—a minute stretched to the verge of breaking until he asks, "When?"

"Not for a very long time," I promise, planting too many wet kisses on his cheeks.

Prone to ticklishness, usually, my son would laugh. Instead, he shifts from me, this new wisdom already tugging him out of childhood, making him a little less my baby. "But your mom, she died when you were little, like Bambi's mom?"

I spot a quiet terror in his expression, the math he must be computing. I was ten when mine died, and he will be ten in two years. I have told him as many stories as my mind has been able to restore, rebuilding my mother the way he does the Lego castles whenever they fall apart—how he has the gravel in her voice, the exact cadence of her laughter, her sneaky sense of humour.

A quiver sits in my throat, waiting to mutate into tears over a glass of wine later. I nod, frantically hoping his next question will be something I can answer—*How many deer are there in the world? Can I go to the park tomorrow? How are animations made?* I cup the duvet around his shoulders and lift it to his chin. I fix his mohawk, which doesn't need any fixing, anything to avoid the question building in his eyes.

Instead, he asks, "Who tucked you in, then?"

UMUBANGA[8]

---

8   OR i stole creations' sketchbook but can not spot the angry red of errors, or
the initial carvings of continents from raging waters, or the erased lines and faded
ghosts to one day be called countries, i found the formula to joy shaped like the heart
of ripened mangoes draining yellow down fat fingers, i found the crayon box with
the colours jumbled to shade my skin this light absorbing hue, i found the snaking
of my tongue birthed at the Benue-Cross rivers, i found my name standing in the
detritus of the Mopane Woodlands, i found myself in the failed hunter's axe, broken
in the bark of all myselves, i memorised the lines, i chant them when this planet
simmers down from time to time yet still, i can not trace the lie you managed to
document simply because you shackled the people you found, that we are the omega
and not the alpha.

PART V

ANOTHER MOTHER DOES NOT COME WHEN YOURS DIES V

When I am 33, I will visit a therapist because mothering has me in shambles every night, assessing, deeming myself a failure. The first day I visit her will be the morning after my eldest slams a door in my face and yells, *I hate you*, through the wood. I remember saying this to my mother, after watching a girl in a Hallmark movie do it and get her way. I hadn't meant it or meant to make her eyes well up as she asked me why I would say that. He doesn't mean it, the way he doesn't mean he actually wants to grow a 2-foot beard. But the memory doesn't help my self-appraisal.

The therapist will tell me, *No*, I was not just an unlovable teenager who still has to earn love by overachieving.

I will nod into my folded palms, bite back the sting of tears, and say, *Sorry*, when they don't comply and fall anyway. I will tell her that I want to mother my two children better and explain all the ways I fall short, confident that the road leads back to my mother, who still sits pretty on the pedestal I left her on when I was ten.

The therapist will ask, *why?* nod at my explanations, and then she will ask, *What if,* maybe the woman who mothered me after mine couldn't was actually the person I was avoiding becoming, every time I saw myself as a bad mother?

This question will suck the air from my throat because I can't say her name still—my mother's sibling who became my pseudo-mother because her sister had been stupid enough to die and shove an antagonistic pre-teen in her custody.

Maybe, I will say to my therapist. And then, I will cry for an hour in my car.

But that is for later after my body finally grows itself and my brain settles down. After the odds bend for me and I get a degree. After I name being touched, *love*, and promise to love, and to honour, and to obey. After the two children, the divorce, a career change and a move to a new country I once saw only through a peephole in my mother's house. After love meets me there and peels me open, until I am soft as pulp again.

Right now, 11 through 15 are a gummed-up mess because memorising my mother's face in her casket, the delicate fall of her lilac suit, and wondering why she was frowning has left my nerves thread-thin, a dishevelled echo of the child I once was.

Right now, I am 11, lying to my pseudo-mom about my grades even though she will see them and call me stupid.

Right now, I am 12, snacking on a slice of bread when she calls me a glutton and warns everyone in the house to watch the bread bin when I am around.

I am 13, and my best friend's 25-year-old brother lets me take a shot of his whiskey. I throw up in the bathroom and have to be rushed to the clinic, where the doctor says not to worry, that I am just hungover. Right now, my pseudo-mom is smirking, saying she knew it, and what else was I good for?

Right now, I am 14, sneaking out at night to kiss a boy in the shrubs that frame a shortcut between school and home. I hold the feeling of ceaseless flailing of wings in my gut and revisit it when my pseudo-mom tells me I will grow up to be a whore.

I am 15, creeping into a nightclub and letting the dizzying music dull the thudding in my head and doing dismally on my grade 12 exams, the final nail.

Mistake after mistake means that I am supposed to dim into the statistics. To become one of the 29 to 48 percent who become adolescent mothers, the 11.03 percent of unemployed youth, or the 94 percent without a University education. But then, a miracle— my father's sister honours a promise she made to her little brother to school me, no matter what. A miracle, just when my future is as bleak as the desert. She recasts my story, this sister, gives me a chance without the foreboding hanging over my head like a noose this time. Or, in my mother's words, But God. And like that I learn to pray again. In whispers and languages lost and regathered. Nothing but *Amen*-ing. Amen. Amen

*

Five years. That's how long I lived under my pseudo-mom. That's only 11 percent of my life so far. Her home, with its velvety seats and chequered yellow kitchen curtains, should be a feeble recollection, like the smell of cocoa butter on my mother's freshly bathed skin. Right?

Five years, like paper held down by a thumb tuck. Only five years. So why do her words still spread like hives across the landscape of my memories?

Why did the language I learnt in her care become my mother tongue—a revolving door of dagger-shaped sentences to pry out and stab myself with in future whenever I make another stupid mistake, like wedding the wrong man at 25, fleeing him at 27 with a barely two-year-old and eight-month-old, quitting a prized first government job, and then trusting that the people I worked for at my next one were friends, not acquaintances?

Why, when I mistabulate at the self-checkout counter, is her breathy, *Little thief,* so crisp in my ear?

On the mornings my husband insists that I sleep in while he gets the kids ready, why can't I? Why do, *I pity the man who will marry you,* and *You are so lazy,* play on a loop?

Failure.

Why do you smell so bad?

I will give you something to cry about, ehn.

More trouble than you are worth.

Sometimes, people ask when I will let it go. *Beats me.* I want to be free of her haunting, not to palpitate when her name flashes on my phone, ten again, words gummed in my throat.

My therapist frames it kinder, the way she does everything she says. She wants to know, in wading through all these memories, what gives me peace.

My children are 11 and 9 now. When we butt heads, and they stand firm in their opinions, my temper is cut in half. Sometimes I shout, and when they say, *You don't have to yell, Mom,* I am as small as a worm because they are right. *I'm sorry,* I always say, because I am. I offer a hug if they want it, grateful every time they take it, and hope the sound of my soothing vibrates in their ears, a thrumming, unexplainable comfort.

In those moments, I think not of my mother but of her sister, in whose eyes I am a pest. I wonder about her screaming, her kissed teeth and slicing words. I wonder if butting heads with a child whom she didn't push out exhausted her so much that everything she said to me was inevitable—just a thing people said to children who weren't theirs.

What about running? my therapist suggests, *you said you liked that, right?*

I nod but don't make eye contact, the way you're supposed to on this side of the Atlantic, so she continues.

Reading? She tries again, the perfect companion to my writing.

I nod.

What about a spiritual practice? Prayer?

I meet her gaze then, with her doe-like, brown eyes, and smile, hoping she finds it convincing. I think of all the *Thank God's*, I've muttered when things should have not gone my way, but the world rearranged itself somehow in my favour. If there is a God, I am the proof, right? I was not supposed to be here, penning this, right? I was supposed to crumble under the weight of being ripped from my source and then being admonished for being untidy in my grieving. But I am here, right? That's a good thing. Even if peace cannot be resurrected. Even if thinking of God feels like watching something through a peephole, an unreachable thing.

To her, I mumble a, *Yes, prayer.*

Listen, she says softly. *Motherhood isn't something you can quantify. You only have to get it right 75 percent of the time.* The words sound right, are just right—something my mother would secretly say to me about a grade on a test while my father was raging about me not being first in my class. But the gap in my core is moulded around my mother's voice, not an apparition of it.

This is our tenth session, my therapist and I, and my husband assures me that I am doing better that the depression is receding.

I smile at her. *Thank you.* And then I walk back to my car, where habit once again demands that I cry for an hour.

Mummy, please—

ACKNOWLEDGMENTS

When I first came to poetry and essay writing, through classes at Hamline University, to satisfy the requirements of my MFA, this book wasn't even a dream. I am here, and the book is here now, thanks to so many people who have believed in my words, and in so doing, infused me with the same belief. And because many people held my hand, the thanks should be just as long.

Thank you to my professors, Maureen Aitken, Erin Sharkey, and Anna Meek, who showed me the way by introducing me to so many wonderful books.

Thank you to my professor–mentor and now friend, Sheila O'Connor, for seeing the poetry before I did, for writing *Evidence of V* which showed what was possible, for reading all of my words, and for encouraging me along the way.

Thank you to the editors at *The Tusculum Review, Passengers Journal, Contemporary Verse 2, Isele Magazine, Action Spectacle, The Good Life Review* and *Menelique* for reading, generously editing, accepting and publishing some of these poems in their first iterations.

Thank you to professor Richard Pelster-Wiebe, whose kindness and generosity provided the first space in which I ventured beyond my mother tongue-fiction.

Thank you to my literary siblings. The landing is softer because of your companionship—Cheswayo Mphanza, Foday Mannah, Frances Ogamba, Theresa Sylvester, Rešoketšwe Manenzhe & Sihle Ntuli.

Thank you to my first readers, Lenganji Haakantu and Fiske Serah Nyirongo.

Thank you to the best three—my husband and our two children, who are my biggest cheerleaders.

And my mother, the beginning, thank you.

ABOUT THE AUTHOR

Mubanga is a Zambian attorney, editor, and writer. She is the author of *The Mourning Bird* (Jacana), *unmarked graves* (Tusculum University Press), *Obligations to the Wounded* (University of Pittsburgh Press), *Another Mother Does Not Come When Yours Dies* (Wayfarer Books) and *Shipikisha* (forthcoming from Dzanc Books). She is also the winner of the Drue Heinz Literature Prize (2024), selected by Angie Cruz; the Tusculum Review Poetry Chapbook Contest (2022), selected by Carmen Giménez; the Dinaane Debut Fiction Award (2019) & Kalemba Short Story Prize (2019). Her work has appeared or is forthcoming in *Overland, adda, Waxwing, Contemporary Verse 2*, on Netflix, and elsewhere. Her creative practice has received support from the Young African Leadership Initiative, the Hubert H. Humphrey (Fulbright) Fellowship, the Hawkinson Scholarship for Peace and Justice, the Africa Institute and the Mercatus Center at George Mason University. She has an MFA in creative writing from Hamline University, is the founding editor of Ubwali Literary Magazine, a 2024 Miles Morland Scholar, and a PhD student and Interdisciplinary Center for the Study of Global Change (ICGC) scholar at the University of Minnesota Twin Cities.

At Wayfarer Books we believe poetry is the language of the earth. We believe words—shaped like rivers through wild places—can change the shape of the world. We publish poets and writers and renegades who stand outside of mainstream culture—poets, essayists, and storytellers whose work might withstand the scrutiny of crows and coyotes, those who are cryptic and floral, the crepuscular, and the queer-at-heart. We are more than just a publisher but a community of writers. Our mission is to produce books that can serve as a compass and map to all wayfarers through wild terrain.

wayfarerbooks.org

www.ingramcontent.com/pod-product-compliance
Lightning Source LLC
Chambersburg PA
CBHW020419130626
46549CB00006B/2640